NOLAN RYAN

THE RYAN EXPRESS

Nolan Ryan is congratulated by his Texas Rangers teammates after pitching his sixth no-hitter.

NOLAN RYAN

THE RYAN EXPRESS

By Ken Rappoport

DILLON PRESS
New York

Maxwell Macmillan Canada
Toronto

Maxwell Macmillan International
New York   Oxford   Singapore   Sydney

For Bernice,
who makes mere beauty seem dull.

Photo Credits

All photos courtesy of AP—Wide World Photos

Library of Congress Cataloging-in Publication Data

Rappoport, Ken.
  Nolan Ryan: the Ryan Express / Ken Rappoport. — 1st ed.
    p. cm. — (Taking part)
  Summary: A biography of Nolan Ryan, the pitcher for the Texas Rangers who is the all-time leader in no-hitters and strikeouts.
    ISBN 0-87518-524-X
    1. Ryan, Nolan, 1947- —Juvenile literature. 2. Baseball players—United States—Biography—Juvenile literature. [1. Ryan, Nolan, 1947- . 2. Baseball players.] I. Title. II. Series.
GV865.R9R37 1992   796.357'092—dc20   92-3244
[B]

Dillon Press   Maxwell Macmillan Canada, Inc.
Macmillan Publishing Company   1200 Eglinton Avenue East
866 Third Avenue   Suite 200
New York, NY 10022   Don Mills, Ontario M3C 3N1

Macmillan Publishing Company is part of the Maxwell Communication Group of Companies

First Edition

Printed in the United States of America

  10 9 8 7 6 5 4 3 2 1

Contents

Preface

For four decades, baseball fans have enjoyed watching Nolan Ryan on the mound. The same cannot be said of the hitters who have faced his blazing fastball.

Ryan has thrown the fastest pitch ever recorded. He is the all-time leader in no-hitters and strikeouts. He is the only pitcher who has struck out more than 2,000 batters in both the National and American leagues.

Also remarkable is Ryan's staying power. In 1991 he completed his 25th season in the major leagues. At the baseball-ancient age of 44, he proved by pitching his seventh no-hitter that the sport isn't only a young man's game.

No wonder so many people in baseball hold Nolan Ryan in awe. To many in his profession, Ryan is a baseball miracle worker.

INTRODUCTION

Nolan Ryan was an out away from a no-hitter in a 1973 game when the batter stepped up to the plate.

"Hey, you can't use that!" umpire Ron Luciano yelled.

The grinning batter was swinging a long, broad, wooden table leg. "I can't hit him with a regular bat," he replied.

When he came back with his regulation bat, the batter became just another Ryan victim that day. And Ryan had his no-hitter.

In 1991 Nolan Ryan was still throwing no-hitters. After pitching his seventh—three more than anyone else in baseball history—Ryan received this one-word telegram from President George Bush: "Wow!"

It's easy to see why Nolan Ryan's performances have made even presidents speechless.

In the 1960s Ryan was a young sensation who threw harder than anyone in baseball. Four decades later—after over 300 victories, 5,000 strikeouts, and about 100,000

Nolan Ryan winds up for a pitch.

pitches—"The Ryan Express" is still rolling strong.

Fastball pitchers usually have short careers because of the stress that hard throwing puts on their arms. But Ryan has defied the odds. Now in his 40s, he is a better pitcher than he was in his 20s. And he still throws as hard as anyone in baseball.

Slugger Reggie Jackson struck out 22 times against Ryan. He paid this tribute to the most remarkable pitcher of our time: "Nolan Ryan was the only pitcher I was ever scared to face."

COUNTRY BOY

The blazing Texas sun beat down on Nolan Ryan as he walked to the mound for the Alvin High School Yellowjackets. Tall and skinny, all arms and legs on a stick of a body, Ryan was a pitcher on a mission. He threw some warm-up shots, squeezed a resin bag, and signaled that he was ready.

The crowd quieted as Ryan looked in for the sign, then went into his delivery motion. He tucked his head into his chest as he whipped his arms up, then kicked his left leg chin-high. In one fluid motion, he brought his arms down and threw the ball with a straight overhand delivery from behind his ear. The ball whizzed past the head of the startled batter, sailing wildly into the backdrop.

"Ball one!" the umpire cried.

Ryan managed a tight smile. He went into his motion again. The ball whistled over the plate.

"Strike one!"

Watching the hard-throwing young pitcher was Red

Nolan Ryan speaks to reporters after his 300th win.

Murff, a scout for the New York Mets. Murff was awe-struck by the speed of Ryan's pitches. He could also see that the batters were frightened by Ryan's wildness.

They were swinging at bad pitches, it seemed, just to get out of there. And the good pitches were so fast they were unhittable.

Later Murff excitedly told the Mets: "This skinny right-handed junior has the best arm I've ever seen in my life."

Murff's report and his faith in Nolan Ryan put the young pitcher from Texas on the road to the major leagues. Twenty years later Ryan would return to play in his home state—as one of baseball's greatest pitchers.

Lynn Nolan Ryan, Jr., was born on January 31, 1947, in Refugio, Texas. His father's family had originally come from Ireland and had lived in Texas for over a hundred years. His mother, Martha Lee Hancock, was said to be related to John Hancock, one of the signers of the Declaration of Independence.

When Ryan was six weeks old, his family moved to Alvin, a small quiet town about 30 miles from Houston. There wasn't much to do for excitement in Alvin. As a boy, Ryan sometimes headed with his friends for the bayou, a swamplike body of water. On hot and humid summer days, the boys would search for water moccasins, poisonous snakes that lived in the murky water. With great excitement, they'd throw stones at the distant, squirming snakes. Yelps of joy would erupt when they scored direct hits on their targets.

Throwing—and connecting with a target—came naturally to young Ryan.

"I was throwing something or other all the time," he later said. "My mother was constantly on me about breaking windows."

Ryan put his throwing arm to better use at age nine when he joined Little League. Within a couple of years, he had pitched his first no-hitter, played just about every position, and made the all-star team.

"I was successful," Ryan remembered, "but not superior to the other kids. I could always throw farther that the other kids—not harder, just farther."

Young Ryan worked hard to improve his baseball skills. Hard work, like throwing, came naturally to the boy. In large part, that was due to the example set by his father.

Lynn Nolan Ryan, Sr., a tall, athletic-looking man, was a supervisor for an oil company. He also worked a second job delivering newspapers to earn extra income to send his six children to college.

Everyone in the family helped with the newspaper route: Nolan; his brother, Robert; and his sisters, Lynda, Mary Lou, Judy, and Jean.

Many mornings Nolan would get up at one o'clock and walk down the dark streets toward the large building on the corner to join his dad. Inside, stacks of newspapers filled the room. Nolan picked up copies of the *Houston Post* and skillfully rolled and tied them. He could roll a stack of 50 papers in five minutes. The boy developed strong hands tying the papers. This helped him as a pitcher.

Nolan helped with the deliveries before going home to catch a few hours of sleep.

"My father's dedication to [earning] that extra income taught me the pride of doing all you can," Nolan said.

Pride and dedication showed in all young Ryan did: schoolwork, playing baseball, helping his dad...even raising cattle.

Nolan feeds some of the beefmaster bulls that live on his ranch in Alvin, Texas.

Ryan loved animals. He thought the he might someday like to be a veterinarian or cattle farmer. When he was 12 years old he bought his first calf, for $2.50.

Ryan kept his calf in a pasture outside town, where he

would go each day to feed it. When a storm or hurricane threatened, Ryan brought the calf home to the safety of his garage. As the storm exploded around them, Ryan would sit quietly in the dark garage, feeding the calf milk from a baby bottle to keep him calm.

While Ryan knew how to be gentle with his pets, he could also be brave. Carrying an empty pan one day, he started for the pasture. He planned to gather blackberries, the calf's favorite treat. As always, his dog, Suzy, was at his side.

All of a sudden, a pack of ferocious dogs stood in their way. Growling and threatening, the dogs started toward Ryan and Suzy.

Suzy stood trembling. The lead dog made his move. Ryan smashed the empty pan against the fierce dog's snout. The dog was so surprised and dazed that Ryan was able to grab Suzy and run off. His pan was bent out of shape, but he had saved his dog.

Ryan's love of animals was soon joined by another passion: basketball.

"All I thought about in high school was basketball," he later said. A center on the Alvin High team, Ryan dreamed of playing basketball in college. He never did. On the day that a local college held basketball tryouts, Ryan was scheduled to pitch for the baseball team.

Ryan was short for a center—only 6'2"—but he played the position because he could jump. He led the Yellowjackets to 27-4 records in each of his junior and senior years.

Ryan also was an ace at a popular game in the Alvin High gym class called "Bombardment." Here's how it worked: Two teams stood at opposite sides of the gym, with volleyballs lined up in the middle. The coach blew his whistle, and there was a free-for-all stampede for the balls. The rule: Throw a ball and hit someone on the opposite team, and the target was out of the game.

When Ryan got the ball, the other players scrambled for the corners. Ryan hit hard, and nobody wanted to be around when he threw.

Ryan could not only throw hard but far. When he participated in his school's presidential exercise program, he would throw a softball. While other students, if they were lucky, threw the ball 50 yards, Ryan threw it 100 yards.

Ryan's throwing ability also helped him excel at baseball.

A rare sight—Nolan Ryan argues with the home plate umpire about a call.

Even though basketball was his favorite sport in high school, Ryan was a star on the baseball team. Ryan was wild, but when he got the ball over the plate he was usually untouchable.

In his senior year, Ryan won 20 games and lost only 4. He was selected for the all-state team and led the Yellowjackets to the state tournament, where he pitched a no-hitter.

Ryan enjoyed watching baseball, too. He and his friends sometimes drove to the Houston Astrodome to watch the major leaguers play. Ryan was a big fan of Sandy Koufax, the great left-handed Dodger. But watching Koufax pitch, Ryan believed, was the closest he would ever come to the major leagues.

2

METS MISERY

The tension was thick as Nolan Ryan faced the biggest decision of his life.

On his kitchen table was a $30,000 contract from the New York Mets. A pen sat on top.

Thirty thousand dollars! That was more money than anyone in the Ryan family had ever seen. Nolan's father worked two jobs. And now Nolan, the youngest of the Ryan clan, had the opportunity to make more money than his father—just by playing ball.

Nolan knew that his father wanted him to sign. He respected his dad more than anyone else in the world.

But Nolan wasn't sure that he wanted to be a professional baseball player. Yes, he enjoyed baseball and had made a reputation for himself as Alvin High School's best pitcher. But he had dreamed of going to college to play basketball. Or to one day become a cattle farmer or a veterinarian.

All these thoughts crossed Nolan's mind as he sat at the

Young Nolan Ryan reports for spring training at the Mets training camp. 21

kitchen table, expectant faces watching.

Finally a voice shattered the silence. It was Steve Vernon, a sportswriter from Texas City who had been invited to sit in on the signing.

"My God, young man, that man [Mets scout Red Murff] is offering you a sizable amount of money to go and play a game," Vernon said. "I'd sign if I were you."

Nolan signed.

The date was June 28, 1965, a historic occasion, as it would turn out. But at the time Ryan was just another 18-year-old who had signed a professional baseball contract.

For Ryan, signing that contract meant a major change in his life-style. He had never been away from home. The plane ride he took from Texas to join the Mets minor league team in Marion, Virginia, was the first he had ever taken in his life. In Marion, Ryan was homesick, lonely, and, he recalled, "scared to death."

But perhaps not as scared as some minor league batters when they faced his often-wild fastball. The hitters feared for their safety, and so did the fans. While playing with Greenville in 1966, a Ryan pitch hit a fan sitting behind home plate. At the next game the woman was sitting all the way back in the stands.

When he got the ball over the plate, Ryan could be unhittable. A pitcher who averages one strikeout per inning pitched is considered exceptional. In three seasons, Ryan had 445 strikeouts in 291 innings—an average of over one and a half per inning.

The Mets could not ignore this remarkable talent. They brought Ryan up to the majors briefly in 1966, after he had pitched in only 45 professional games. Then in 1968, Ryan was back in the majors to stay.

The young pitcher had blazed his way into the major leagues through his natural abilities. But his inexperience showed. So did his control problems.

He established a dubious Met record by walking eight batters in one game. In another, he walked the opposing pitcher with the bases loaded. That was considered a baseball "sin," since pitchers are usually the weakest hitters in the lineup.

"I lost my confidence in myself, even in my fastball," Ryan said. "The Mets were fighting for a pennant. They couldn't afford to work out my control problems."

Those weren't the only problems Ryan had. Many physical ailments—a sore arm, pulled groin muscle, and blisters on his pitching hand—plagued the young hurler. Ryan's pitching was also interrupted by Army Reserve meetings and summer camp, which kept him from playing regularly.

The blisters were caused by a childhood accident. Ryan had tried to turn the top of a coffee can that was partially slit. He cut the thumb, middle, and ring fingers of his right hand. "The scar tissue built up, and throwing a baseball, it led to blisters," Ryan said.

The blisters hurt Ryan's performance. He tried any solution to cure them, including bathing his hand in pickle brine to toughen the skin (an idea of Mets trainer Gus Mauch). It didn't do much good.

When he wasn't in Texas for Army Reserve meetings or on the disabled list with an injury, Ryan was usually sitting unhappily in the Mets bullpen. He came into games occasionally as a relief pitcher, usually when there was little at stake. He felt like the forgotten man on the Mets' pitching staff.

Ryan complained that this inactivity ruined his pitching

Ryan fires one down the line in a 1968 game against the Los Angeles Dodgers.

"rhythm," and his record reflected that. Ryan could be brilliant at times—as he was when he struck out a club-record 14 batters in one game, then bettered that with a 15-strikeout performance in another game. But too often, Ryan struggled. He lost more games than he won for the Mets. But Ryan didn't stop trying his hardest.

One of Ryan's few good moments as a relief pitcher came in the 1969 World Series against the Baltimore Orioles.

The bases were loaded in the ninth inning of Game Three. At bat was the dangerous Paul Blair, who had hit a long drive off Ryan in the seventh inning. Ryan reared back and released his fastball. He got two quick strikes on Blair.

Then Ryan threw a curveball. The surprised Blair never got the bat off his shoulder.

The umpire had barely gotten out the words "Strike three!" before Ryan was mobbed by his teammates. The fans at Shea Stadium were on their feet, cheering and applauding. Ryan had the save and the "Amazin' Mets" took a 2-1 lead in the Series they would eventually win.

It was a proud moment for Ryan. But it didn't change his feelings about the Mets and their city. Ryan didn't like

A young fan proudly displays his trophy, a Nolan Ryan rookie card from the 1968 Mets.

living in New York. After the 1971 season he told the Mets, "If you don't trade me, I'm going to quit baseball and go back to Texas."

Ryan got his wish to be traded—but it was to the last place he expected.

3

AN ANGEL
ON HIS SHOULDER

Nolan Ryan was shocked. He had expected to stay in the National League and hoped to play with the Houston Astros in Texas in 1972. Instead, he had been traded to the American League's California Angels.

Questions raced through Ryan's mind as he packed for spring training. What would it be like living in California? Playing in the American League? He knew some things about the Angels, none of them very good: They had a losing record in 1971; they drew small crowds; and they were overshadowed by the Los Angeles Dodgers and Disneyland in Southern California. Ryan also had to wonder about the shocking news that one of the players had been found with a gun in the clubhouse.

Ryan joined the Angels with doubts, and these doubts doubled as he struggled with his control in spring training. The harder he tried, the wilder he became. In one exhibition game, one of Ryan's pitches struck a San Francisco batter

Nolan shows off his new California Angels uniform.

and sparked a brawl with the Giants.

Times got worse when a players' strike canceled some exhibition and early season games. The Ryans had to borrow money to get to California in the first place, then they had to borrow more to live during the strike. There was another mouth to feed as well: Ryan's wife, Ruth, had given birth to their first son, Reid. There was no money coming into the Ryan household.

It was, as Ryan would later remember, the lowest point of his career. Ryan considered his first spring training with the Angels a disaster, and he was so discouraged that he thought again about quitting baseball. But Ruth Ryan—the childhood sweetheart he had married five years earlier—convinced him to stay.

Luckily the strike only lasted 12 days, and Ryan was happy he wasn't a quitter. All he needed was regular work, and he got plenty of that with the Angels. Ryan had a regular spot in the pitching rotation. The Angels' coaches and catchers, particularly pitching coach Tom Morgan and catcher Jeff Torborg, worked with him on his pitching mechanics. Ryan worked extra hours to alter his delivery and improved his

Ryan demonstrates the grip that helped him break Sandy Koufax's strikeout record.

curveball and change-up, a pitch that reached home plate more slowly than his blinding fastball.

The improvement was dramatic. In Ryan's four previous seasons in New York, he had won a total of only 29 games. In his first season in California, he won a career-high 19.

His second season in California brought two no-hitters and one of the biggest challenges of his career.

It was September 26, 1973. Ryan was pitching in his last game of the season, against the Minnesota Twins. For weeks, he had been closing in on Sandy Koufax's season record of 382 strikeouts. He needed 16 strikeouts against the Twins to break the record.

By the fifth inning, he had 12. In the seventh inning, he tied the record with his 15th strikeout.

The fans at Anaheim Stadium had been cheering each strike and booing every ball the Twins hit fair. Now Ryan received a huge ovation.

Everyone in the ballpark was waiting for Ryan to break the record.

He failed to strike out a batter in the eighth inning.

And again in the ninth.

Nolan tags out a runner at first.

But the game was tied, and he still had a chance at the record in extra innings.

Ryan went into the 10th inning suffering from exhaustion and leg cramps. Somehow he found the strength to get through the inning. But still no record-breaking strikeout.

In the 11th inning, the exhausted pitcher got two outs— neither of them strikeouts—and walked Rod Carew.

Then came Rich Reese, who might be his last chance. Ryan threw as hard as he could. Reese swung and missed.

Ryan looked over his shoulder at first base to keep Carew close, then fired a pitch that Reese missed. Strike two!

Carew had taken off for second base on the pitch. Torborg instinctively ripped off his mask and fired across the diamond, trying to get the runner. Too late: Carew was safe.

Torborg said later that he was relieved he had not thrown out Carew, because that would have been the third out and it would have denied Ryan the strikeout record.

Ryan didn't have much strength left, but whatever he had he put into his next pitch. Reese swung from the heels— and missed!

Ryan had the record-breaking strikeout!

Anaheim Stadium was bedlam as the fans, hoarse from screaming throughout the game, stood and applauded for five minutes. Ryan's teammates swarmed around him, shaking his hand and slapping his back.

In the bottom of the inning, the Angels scored the winning run. Ryan not only had the strikeout record but his 21st victory of the season as well.

Over the next two years, Ryan pitched two more no-hitters for the Angels, tying Sandy Koufax's record of four. Sometimes Ryan's pitches weren't just impossible to hit—they were too fast to see! Batters talked about "hearing" Ryan's pitches. "That sounded low" or "That sounded high," they would say.

The record for baseball's fastest pitch had been set by Bob Feller in 1946 at 98.6 miles per hour. In 1974 Nolan Ryan broke that long-standing record in a game against the Chicago White Sox at Anaheim Stadium.

The Angels got the most out of the occasion. They sponsored a contest offering a free trip to Hawaii for the fan who could guess Ryan's fastest pitch.

Ryan didn't enjoy pitching in the carnival-like atmosphere. Everyone seemed more interested in how fast Ryan would throw, not if the Angels won or lost.

The Angels brought in top scientists with sophisticated electronic equipment. They were positioned in the press box. There they shot down a beam of light over home plate to measure the speed of Ryan's pitches.

They didn't measure every pitch, but they did time seven of them at over 100 miles per hour—including the one that set the record in the ninth inning.

White Sox shortstop Bee Bee Richard stepped up to the plate. Ryan unleashed his fastball and Richard swung and missed.

The batter turned around to Angels catcher Tom Egan.

"Where was that?" he asked Egan.

"Well, it was right down the middle," Egan said.

"Jeez," said Richard. "I didn't even see it."

The ball was timed at 101.8 miles per hour, beating Feller's record by a large margin. (In less official circumstances in an earlier game against the Detroit Tigers, Ryan was timed even faster: at 101.9.)

By 1979, Ryan had played eight great seasons with

the Angels. The fans loved him, and everyone on the team looked up to him. Ryan hoped to remain with the Angels for the rest of his baseball career, but he didn't count on a bitter contract dispute.

Buzzie Bavasi had replaced Harry Dalton as the Angels' general manager. His lack of respect in contract negotiations angered Ryan. Ryan was insulted when Bavasi said he could replace him with two pitchers with 8-7 records (Ryan was 16-14 with the Angels in 1979).

At the end of the season, Ryan packed his bags. He knew he would never come back to the Angels. But he had no idea where he was going next.

4

STRIKING IT RICH

"Welcome back to Texas."

The sign said it all. Thousands cheered on a cold December day in 1979 as Nolan Ryan came up the main street of Alvin.

Ryan had signed a contract with the Houston Astros. "I've thought about this moment for many years and dreamed about it growing up in Alvin," Ryan said. "I always wanted to play for the Astros and live at home."

Ryan's contract caused almost as much attention as his return home. The Astros were paying him $1 million a year. At that time, nobody had ever been paid that much in any team sport. Was a baseball player worth all that money?

To the Astros he was. Ryan was the biggest drawing card in baseball. Pitching before his hometown fans, he would be worth his weight in gate receipts.

For Ryan, the contract was the payoff to a big gamble. He was 32 years old, reaching an age when many baseball

Nolan Ryan greets the crowd in one of his first games as a member of the Houston Astros.

players retire. He had left California uncertain how many teams would be interested in him and willing to pay the kind of money he thought he was worth.

As it turned out, many teams were interested, including the Astros. There was no question about which team's offer he would accept.

Ryan had become notable in California for pitching no-hitters. The Astros hoped their new pitcher had a few no-hitters left in his arm. So did Ryan.

Since tying Sandy Koufax's record with his fourth no-hitter in 1975, he had tried in vain for a record-breaking fifth. Too many times he had come close, only to be frustrated. He was starting to feel that at his age, he might never pitch a no-hitter again.

Ryan usually did not care much about records. But Koufax was his boyhood hero, and breaking his no-hit record would be a special triumph.

On September 26, 1981, Ryan faced the Los Angeles Dodgers in a big game. The ingredients were there for high drama. The Astros and Dodgers were fighting for the lead in the National League West. The crucial Saturday afternoon

Nolan traded his chewing tobacco for bubble gum after seeing young fans using tobacco to imitate their baseball heroes.

game at the Houston Astrodome was being shown on national television.

From the first inning, Ryan was in top form, setting down batter after batter. Six innings—and the Dodgers had not come close to a hit. Then in the seventh, Mike Scioscia hit a long drive to right center field. Right fielder Terry Puhl, running at the crack of the bat, raced back toward the wall.

The crowd held its breath, hoping that this would not be another failed attempt at the record.

With many of the fans on their feet, Puhl plucked the ball out of the air to keep Ryan's no-hitter alive.

Tension was building. The crowd cheered with every pitch.

In the ninth, Ryan struck out pinch hitter Reggie Smith. Ken Landreaux was next. The count went to three balls and one strike before Landreaux grounded out to first base for the second out. Just one more to go.

Now many of the fans were on their feet, screaming.

Dusty Baker, the Dodgers' leading batter and a good fastball hitter, was the last man to stand between Ryan and the no-hitter.

Ryan threw Baker curveballs. Baker hit one on the ground to third base. Art Howe fielded the ball cleanly and threw Baker out to complete the no-hitter, breaking Koufax's record.

Ryan's teammates, as excited as their pitcher, lifted him onto their shoulders and carried him off the field. Nolan Ryan was baseball's no-hit king.

The game was a trademark Ryan performance. Ryan had not only pitched his fifth no-hitter; he had also added 11 strikeouts to his total. By the end of the season, he had well over 3,000 strikeouts.

Nolan Ryan was in a position to become baseball's all-time strikeout leader. But so were Gaylord Perry and Steve Carlton. Who would do it first?

5

STRIKEOUT WHIZ

Nolan Ryan was never much into baseball history—until he started making some himself.

Going into the 1982 season, Ryan was thinking about Walter Johnson. Pitching for the old Washington Senators, Johnson had struck out a record 3,508 batters before finishing his career in 1927.

Gaylord Perry of the Seattle Mariners was second on the all-time strikeout list, Ryan of the Houston Astros was third, and Steve Carlton of the Philadelphia Phillies was fourth. It was a race among the three to see who would be the first to break Johnson's record.

In 1982, Ryan struck out 245 to take the lead, with 3,494 strikeouts. Now he needed 15 to break the record. Before the 1983 season, Ryan bought a baseball encyclopedia to brush up on Johnson's records. He also did some reading about Johnson and discovered that he had a lot in common with the great Washington pitcher.

Nolan Ryan throws another strike on his way to breaking Walter Johnson's record.

Like Ryan, Johnson had been recognized as the fastest pitcher of his day. The two great pitchers' nicknames are similar: Johnson was called "The Big Train"; Ryan, "The Ryan Express."

Johnson's fastball was so frightening that the kindhearted pitcher avoided throwing brushback pitches—a ball thrown close to the batter's head to scare him off the plate. Similarly, Ryan will not deliberately throw near a batter's head.

Johnson had died in 1946. Ryan was born in 1947. Both men had similar physiques—tall and slim—and small-town backgrounds. Both preferred a quiet country life to big-city lights.

When Johnson retired from baseball, he became a farmer and raised milk cows. Ryan raises cattle in Texas during the off-season. He owns thousands of acres of ranchland. There he rides the range and brands cattle, just like a cowboy out of the Old West.

Johnson, good-natured and easygoing, was known as one of baseball's great gentlemen. So is Ryan. Because of their regard for Ryan, several teammates have named sons after him.

Nolan talks with a teammate after coming one step closer to setting the strikeout record.

They aren't the only ones who have high regard for Ryan's character. He is in high demand by advertisers who seek his endorsement because of his honesty and sincerity. Ryan appears regularly in national magazines and on television.

As a cattleman and owner of a Texas bank, he has become a successful businessman, admired by his fellow townspeople. But Ryan remembers when times were tougher, and in the off-season he was pumping gas instead of riding the range. Today Ryan is careful how he spends his own money, and he manages the bank's money with equal care.

Both Johnson and Ryan have been role models for young fans. Johnson didn't smoke, swear, or drink, and Ryan is also clean-living. He stopped chewing tobacco when he saw Little Leaguers near his hometown imitating the big leaguers by playing with their cheeks full of chaw. He shows his appreciation for his young fans in other ways, too.

Leaving the Houston Astrodome once with some friends for a hunting trip, Ryan spotted a group of youngsters. He told his friends he would join them later. After signing autographs he did join them—two hours later.

Both Johnson and Ryan have had presidential admirers. President Calvin Coolidge declared Johnson a natural role model for young fans. President George Bush said Ryan was "a top human being and a top performer...a great symbol for kids around this country that love baseball as much as I do."

Ryan was struck by all the similarities between himself and the legendary strikeout king. His excitement built as he entered the 1983 season.

But things started slowly for him. Because of various aches and pains, Ryan didn't get to pitch much in spring training.

Not even Ryan's special homemade "snake oil remedy" could help. He had been using homemade remedies since his days with the New York Mets, when he soaked his hand in pickle brine to try to cure a blister problem. When he was with the California Angels, Ryan used snake oil, made from snakes he'd caught in the wild, to cure aches and pains. His Angel teammates had started calling him "Dr. Snake Oil."

Ryan missed several games early in the 1983 season when he was hospitalized for prostatitis (an inflammation of the prostate gland). It was yet another health problem for

Ryan to overcome. He has faced many during his career: blisters on his fingers, bone chips in his elbow, a stress fracture in his lower back, a torn ligament in his arm, groin pulls and tendinitis (an inflammation of tendons in his arms and legs), among others.

Rarely have these ailments kept him from pitching. Nor have injuries. A ball hit by Kansas City's Bo Jackson opened a two-inch gash on Ryan's lower lip. The gash wouldn't stop bleeding, but Ryan wouldn't stop pitching. His uniform became so bloody that he was forced to change twice. In a similar situation when he was in high school, Ryan was knocked out by a batted ball. When he came to, he refused to stop pitching and finished the game.

Ryan had been especially anxious to get going in the 1983 season. But because of his health problems, he didn't get his first start until the 12th game of the season. Then he struck out seven batters. In his next start he added three to leave him five short of the all-time strikeout record.

On April 27, Ryan stood on the mound at Montreal's Olympic Stadium as the Astros faced the Montreal Expos. He failed to get a strikeout in the first inning. He got two in the

Nolan shows off the powerhouse style that made him baseball's strikeout king.

second and another in the sixth.

In the eighth inning Ryan tied Johnson's strikeout record, punching out Tim Blackwell on a fastball for number 3,508. Now he was one strikeout away from replacing Walter Johnson as the all-time strikeout leader.

Brad Mills, a substitute infielder for the Expos, was at the plate. In their only previous meeting, the season before, Mills had managed to get a base hit off Ryan.

Ryan walked around the back of the mound, telling himself not to rush his delivery. Then he braced himself on the rubber and fired a fastball over the outside corner of the plate for a strike.

Ryan's second pitch was a curveball. Mills swung and missed. Strike two.

Ryan wasted a fastball outside, then walked off the mound and yanked at his cap. He squeezed the ball, braced on the rubber, and looked in for the sign from catcher Alan Ashby.

He raised his arms over his head, tucked his leg into his chest, rocked on the mound, and threw a big breaking curveball over the outside corner of the plate.

Mills was frozen.

"Strike three!" umpire Bob Engel cried as he turned and threw a hard jab in the air, marking the memorable occasion.

More than 19,000 fans rose to cheer Ryan's record-breaking strikeout. The pitcher hesitantly raised his orange Astros cap. His likeness appeared along with Johnson's on the giant electronic scoreboard in the center field.

When the inning was over, Ryan quietly shook hands with his teammates, then sat down in the dugout to cool off.

"To him, it was a relief to get it over with," Ashby said. "He was getting annoyed with reporters coming up for weeks asking about the situation. Now he could get back to playing."

6

LONE STAR LEGEND

Nolan Ryan had just finished pitching his seventh no-hitter. But this was no time to rest. With an ice pack strapped to his arm, he climbed onto his exercise bike in the conditioning room and began pedaling furiously.

Music blared from a radio in a corner of the locker room. Camera flashguns exploded and television lights flooded the room. Ryan's Texas Rangers teammates laughed, swapped jokes, and talked to reporters.

Sweat streamed down Ryan's face as he continued to pedal.

"Does this guy ever quit?" one reporter asked.

The answer is no.

Ryan, a fitness fanatic, has been following the same exercise program for many years: sweaty hours of pedaling, running, stretching, and lifting weights in between pitching assignments and during the off-season. His work ethic has become legendary in baseball.

Nolan Ryan proudly shows off the cap of his new team, the Texas Rangers.

"He's as hard working a player as I've ever seen," said Jeff Torborg, manager of the New York Mets, who was once Ryan's teammate. "You can't work any harder than Nolan does."

Ryan joined the Texas Rangers in 1989. He immediately set a work standard in spring training. He wasn't satisfied just to pitch a game. Off the mound, he worked just as hard. There was an outside staircase near the Rangers' clubhouse along the right-field line. In between innings, Ryan walked up and down the stairs, exercising his calves.

"He works like crazy to stay ready," says Torborg.

Maybe that explains why Ryan has lasted so long in the major leagues—and has surprised all the teams that gave up on him.

The New York Mets traded Ryan in 1972 when he was a struggling young pitcher. The California Angels let Ryan go in 1980 because they felt he was getting too old to be a consistent winner. The Houston Astros were worried about Ryan's age, too. In 1987 they cut his pitch limit, trying to "save" his arm. After the 1988 season, when the Astros tried to cut his salary, Ryan decided it was time to leave Houston.

Nolan Ryan acknowledges the crowd after winning his 300th game.

Rickey Henderson of the Oakland A's shakes his head in disbelief after giving Nolan Ryan his 5,000th career strikeout.

He had offers from other teams, but he joined the Texas Rangers because he wanted to stay near his family.

In 1990 Ryan was 43 years old, an age at which most players are retired. That year he won his 300th game, to join an exclusive club. Only 19 other pitchers have won that many games in their careers.

The 1990 season became memorable for another reason when Ryan pitched a no-hitter against the Oakland Athletics. He repeated the accomplishment in 1991—his 25th year in the majors—when he pitched his seventh no-hitter, this time against the Toronto Blue Jays. On each occasion, Ryan set new records as the oldest pitcher to throw a no-hitter.

After the no-hitter in Oakland, the pitcher and his family celebrated in typical Ryan fashion: They went back to their hotel room and had pizza. Ryan tries to have his family with him during the baseball season as much as he can.

The 300th victory, like many of Ryan's games, was also a family affair. Watching the game in Milwaukee were Nolan's wife, Ruth, and his children, Wendy, Reid, and Reese.

Reid and Reese sat with their father in the dugout. Reid took family videos while Reese gave his father back rubs. Perhaps remembering that his own hard-working father didn't have much time for his children, Ryan has taken his sons on several road trips with the Rangers.

Few fathers are closer to their children than Ryan is. He has said he considers his obligations as a father much more important than baseball.

When his son Reid was hit by a car in 1979, Ryan spent almost as much time visiting him in the hospital as he did playing baseball. Reid lost his spleen and a kidney. But with trademark Ryan determination, he didn't let the health prob-

Ryan relaxes in the dugout after throwing his sixth career no-hitter.

lems stop him from becoming a baseball player.

In 1991, Nolan and Reid made baseball history when they pitched against each other. In an exhibition game, Reid pitched for the University of Texas and Nolan for the Texas Rangers. The father-son matchup attracted national attention. The Rangers won, but Nolan's loyalties were divided. When Nolan was pitching, he rooted for his own team. When Reid was pitching, Nolan rooted for his son.

For Reid, it was a thrill to pitch against his famous father—and a learning experience as well.

"One thing I learned from him is how to carry myself," Reid said. "To stay collected and cool out there. To act like a professional."

Few sons have ever had a better example to follow. From his dad, Reid has also learned about dedication and determination, courage and character.

Nolan Ryan had to overcome many problems to reach the top. He learned to control his wildness, which nearly finished him as a young pitcher. He was troubled by physical ailments and injuries that continuously interrupted his career. But he came back, time and again, often pitching in pain.

Ryan remembered the lessons that he learned from his own father. Lessons about hard work and a sense of responsibility.

As Ryan got older, teams gave up on him—but he never gave up on himself. They never counted on Ryan's pride and competitive spirit.

Through sheer determination, Nolan Ryan has become one of baseball's greatest pitchers and one of its top attractions. Fans flock to the ballpark whenever Ryan pitches. There's always a chance they will see something spectacular—perhaps another no-hitter or a new strikeout record.

"The Ryan Express" is full speed ahead.

Index

About the Author

Ken Rappoport is a sports writer for the Associated Press. He has covered every major sport, and currently is the AP's national hockey writer.

Ken has authored books on football, baseball, and basketball. He has written about sports and entertainment for national magazines, and received a national award in the 1991 Writer's Digest writing competition.

The author lives in Old Bridge, N.J., with his wife, Bernice, and his father and mother. He has two daughters and a son.